MAGNETS

Do-It-Yourself Experiments

Gina Hagler and John Willis
Illustrated by Bob Ostrom

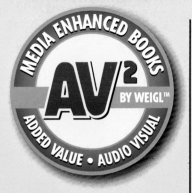

AV² provides enriched content that supplements and complements this book. Weigl's AV² books strive to create inspired learning and engage young minds in a total learning experience.

Your AV² Media Enhanced books come alive with...

Audio
Listen to sections of the book read aloud.

Key Words
Study vocabulary, and complete a matching word activity.

Video
Watch informative video clips.

Quizzes
Test your knowledge.

Embedded Weblinks
Gain additional information for research.

Slide Show
View images and captions, and prepare a presentation.

Try This!
Complete activities and hands-on experiments.

... and much, much more!

Go to **www.av2books.com**, and enter this book's unique code.

BOOK CODE

Q857547

AV² by Weigl brings you media enhanced books that support active learning.

Published by AV² by Weigl
350 5th Avenue, 59th Floor
New York, NY 10118
Website: www.av2books.com

Library of Congress Cataloging-in-Publication Data

Names: Hagler, Gina, author. | Willis, John, 1989- author. | Hagler, Gina. Step-by-step experiments with magnets.
Title: Magnets / Gina Hagler and John Willis.
Description: New York, NY : AV2 by Weigl, [2017] | Series: Do-it-yourself experiments | Previous title: Step-by-step experiments with magnets / by Gina Hagler ; illustrated by Bob Ostrom (Mankato, Minn. : Child's World, c2012). | Includes bibliographical references and index.
Identifiers: LCCN 2016007967 (print) | LCCN 2016008826 (ebook) | ISBN 9781489652867 (hard cover) | ISBN 9781489652874 (soft cover) | ISBN 9781489652881 (multi-user eBook)
Subjects: LCSH: Magnets--Experiments--Juvenile literature. | Magnetism--Experiments--Juvenile literature. | Science projects--Juvenile literature.
Classification: LCC QC753.7 .H34 2017 (print) | LCC QC753.7 (ebook) | DDC 538.078--dc23
LC record available at http://lccn.loc.gov/2016007967

Printed in the United States of America in Brainerd, Minnesota
1 2 3 4 5 6 7 8 9 0 20 19 18 17 16

082016
210716

Project Coordinator: John Willis   Art Director: Terry Paulhus

Every reasonable effort has been made to trace ownership and to obtain permission to reprint copyright material. The publishers would be pleased to have any errors or omissions brought to their attention so that they may be corrected in subsequent printings.

Weigl acknowledges Getty Images and iStock as its primary image suppliers for this title.

2 Do-It-Yourself Experiments

Table of Contents

Have you ever seen alphabet magnets? Magnets can be used to stick paper to a surface or as decoration. Some people even collect magnets.

Study Magnets

Have you seen a magnet stuck to a refrigerator? Magnets stick to some things, such as metal, but they do not stick to everything.

Magnets have two ends. They are called **poles**. One is its north pole. The other is its south pole. A magnetic **force** pushes or pulls magnets. The magnetic force is strongest at a magnet's poles. Opposite poles of magnets **attract**, or pull together. If the poles are the same, magnets **repel**, or push away from each other.

This push and pull makes magnets useful. Toy trains connect with magnets. Some doors pull closed with magnets. Recycling centers use big magnets to pull metal from large trash piles. How can you learn more about magnets?

Seven Science Steps

Doing a science **experiment** is a fun way to discover new facts. An experiment follows steps to find answers to science questions. This book has experiments to help you learn about magnets. You will follow the same seven steps in each experiment.

Seven Steps

1. **Research**
   Figure out the facts before you get started.

2. **Question**
   What do you want to learn?

3. **Guess**
   Make a **prediction**. What do you think
   will happen in the experiment?

4. **Gather**
   Find the supplies you need for your experiment.

5. **Experiment**
   Follow the directions.

6. **Review**
   Look at the results of the experiment.

7. **Conclusion**
   The experiment is done. Now it is
   time to reach a **conclusion**.
   Was your prediction right?

*Are you
ready to become a
scientist? Experiment
to learn
about magnets.*

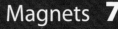

Paper clips come in a lot of different colors and sizes.

Magnet Magic

You can buy many kinds of magnets. Some are shaped like bars. Others have pictures glued to them. Many objects are not magnets, though. Try this to learn if paper clips can become magnets.

Research the Facts

Here are a few. What else do you know?

- Only some things are magnetic. Magnets are usually made of metal.
- A paper clip is made from metal.
- Metal is not always magnetic.

Ask Questions

- Can a magnet make another object magnetic?
- Can metals that are not magnetic become magnets?

Make a Prediction

Here are two examples.
- A magnet can make a paper clip magnetic.
- A magnet cannot make a paper clip magnetic.

Gather Your Supplies

A table

A white sheet of paper

Two large metal paper clips

A bar or horseshoe magnet

A pencil or pen

Paper

Time to Experiment

1. Place the white paper on the table.
2. Place one paper clip on the paper.
3. Place the other paper clip on the paper. Put the ends next to each other. Make them about 0.25 inches (6 centimeters) apart.
4. Record what happens.

5. Pick up one paper clip. Rub the paper clip on the magnet. Only rub in one direction.
6. Place the paper clip back on the paper.
7. Rub the other paper clip with the magnet. Only rub in one direction.
8. Place the second paper clip back in the same place.
9. Record what happens.

✓ Review the Results

What did you see? Did the paper clips move before they were rubbed on the magnet? Did they move after they were rubbed on the magnet? The paper clips did not move the first time they were placed on the paper. After the paper clips were rubbed on the magnet, they moved closer when on the paper.

What Is Your Conclusion?

The paper clips became magnetic when they were rubbed on the magnet. The paper clips contain iron. Metal with **iron** can become magnetized.

Paper clips stick together when they are magnetized.

A paper clip only stays magnetized for a short time. If you rub it longer on the magnet, the paper clip will be magnetic for a longer time.

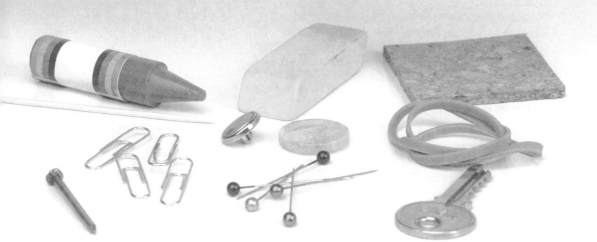

Magnets do not just stick to metal, they can also pick up metal.

Magnetic or Not?

Does everything stick to magnets? Does wood have iron in it? How about plastic? Try this to find out.

Research the Facts

Here are a few. What other facts can you find?
- Magnetic things contain iron.
- Metals are hard and shiny solid objects.

Do magnets attract plastic snap blocks?

Ask Questions

- Is wood, a soda pop can, or plastic magnetic?
- Do both poles of a magnet pull toward magnetic things?

Make a Prediction

Here are two examples.
- Plastic and wood are magnetic.
  They stick to a magnet.
- Plastic and wood are not magnetic.
  They do not stick to a magnet.

Gather Your Supplies.

A few plastic snap blocks

A few pennies

A few small metal paper clips

A few wooden toothpicks

A soda pop can

A plastic container (large enough to hold everything)

A bar magnet (with an N and S marking the poles)

A pencil or pen

Paper

Time to Experiment

1. Place the snap blocks, pennies, soda pop can, paper clips, and toothpicks in the container. Mix them around.
2. Move the south pole of the magnet around in the container. Put it close to the objects.
3. Does anything stick to the magnet? Record what happens.
4. Now, move the north pole of the magnet over the objects. Record what happens.

Paper clips are light enough to be picked up by even a small magnet.

Review the Results

Read your notes. Which objects did not pull to the magnet? What were those objects made of? The pennies and paper clips stuck to both poles of the magnet. The snap blocks, soda pop can, and toothpicks did not stick to either pole of the magnet.

What Is Your Conclusion?

The magnet's poles have the same magnetic force. The pennies and the paper clips contain magnetic things. You can tell because they were pulled toward the magnet. The snap blocks, soda pop can, and toothpicks did not pull. They do not contain magnetic things. Plastic, soda pop cans, and wood are not magnetic.

Soda pop cans are made from aluminum.

FLAVOR SOFT DRINK

FRESH COLA DRINK

Magnetic objects have *iron, nickel, magnetite, or cobalt* in them. A soda pop can is made from aluminum. Aluminum is a metal, but it is not magnetic.

Do Opposites Attract?

Have you felt a toy train's cars pull together? The train has magnets on the end of each car. They attract the other magnets. Sometimes, magnets push away. Why does this happen? In this experiment, you will learn why.

Research the Facts

Here are a few. What other facts do you know?
- Every magnet has a north and a south pole.
- North and south poles are on the opposite ends of a magnet.

Ask Questions
- Do the same poles of two magnets push or pull when touched?
- Do the opposite poles of two magnets push or pull when touched?

Make a Prediction

Here are two examples.
- Opposite poles of two magnets push when put near each other.
- Opposite poles of two magnets pull when put near each other.

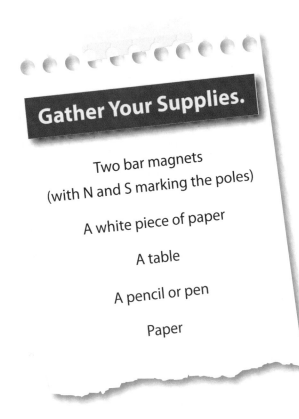

Gather Your Supplies.

Two bar magnets
(with N and S marking the poles)

A white piece of paper

A table

A pencil or pen

Paper

Time to Experiment

1. Place the white paper on the table.
2. Place the two bar magnets on the paper. Put them about 0.25 inches (6 cm) apart. Make sure the same poles face each other.
3. Record what happens.
4. Turn one magnet. Make sure the opposite poles face each other.
5. Record what happens.

 ## Review the Results

Read your notes. What happened when the opposite poles faced each other? What happened when the same poles faced each other? When the two north or south poles faced each other, the magnets pushed apart. When a north and a south pole faced each other, the magnets pulled together.

What Is Your Conclusion?

Opposite poles on a magnet pull toward each other. Even if you push really hard, the same poles of two magnets will not stick together. The force in a magnet points in one direction. It moves in through the south pole and out the north pole. When a south pole touches a north pole, the forces from each pole work together. They make the poles join. When two of the same poles touch, the forces from each work against each other. They push the poles apart.

A toy train connects with the pull of magnets.

The North and South Poles of the globe are magnetic. This is why a compass can always point north.

Chapter 6

Point the Compass

Many people use **compasses** to find their way. They look at the needle on the compass to see where it points. Inside a compass is a magnet. Try this experiment to see how a compass works and where it points.

Research the Facts

Here are a few. What other facts do you know?
- Earth has a **magnetic field**. The magnetic field is between the North and South Poles of Earth.
- A compass needle always points in one direction.

A compass helps you find the direction you want to go.

Ask Questions
- How does a compass work?
- Why is a magnet used in a compass?

Make a Prediction

Here are two examples.
- A compass needle pulls toward Earth's poles.
- A compass needle does not pull toward Earth's poles.

Gather Your Supplies

Adult help

A bar magnet (with N and S marking the poles)

A sewing needle

A bowl

Wax paper

Scissors

Water

A pencil or pen

Paper

Time to Experiment

1. Pour water into the bowl.
2. Cut a circle from the wax paper. Make sure it is small enough to move around in the bowl.
3. Rub one end of the needle on the north pole of the magnet. Rub the needle in one direction, from end to tip. You can ask an adult to help you.

4. Rub the other end
   of the needle on
   the south pole
   of the magnet.
   Rub the needle in
   one direction.
5. Stick the needle
   through the wax paper.
   Push the tip out again
   on the same side.
6. Float the wax paper
   and needle on top of
   the water in the bowl.
   Gently spin the paper.
7. Watch what happens.
   Record what you see.
8. Spin the paper again.
   Where does it stop
   this time? Record
   what you see.

Review the Results

Check out your notes. Did the paper and needle stop spinning? Where did the needle point? Both times, the needle pointed in the same direction.

What Is Your Conclusion?

When a magnet is balanced on something, it will always point to Earth's North and South Poles. The Earth is like a very big magnet. Its force pushes and pulls magnets. The Earth's force goes from its North to South Poles. This makes a compass needle point north.

Way To Go

You are a scientist now. What fun magnet facts did you learn? You found out magnets have opposite poles. You learned that many metals are magnetic. You can learn even more about magnets.

Study it.

Experiment with it.

Then, share what you learn about magnets.

Quiz

1
What are magnets usually made out of?

2
What type of poles pull towards each other?

3
What is inside a compass?

4
How do most toy trains stay together?

5
Can a magnet stick to wood?

6
Where is a magnetic force strongest?

7
How do recycling centers use magnets?

8
What are the poles on a magnet called?

N

S

8. The north and south poles
7. They separate metal from garbage
6. At the magnet's pole
5. No

4. Magnets between the cars
3. A magnet
2. Opposite
1. Metal

Key Words

attract: to pull toward another object

compasses: a tool with a magnetic pointer that shows magnetic north

conclusion: what you learn from doing an experiment

experiment: a test or way to study something to learn facts

force: an action that changes an object's shape or how it moves

iron: a strong, magnetic metal that is silvery gray in appearance

magnetic field: the area around a magnet that has the power to attract other metals

poles: the opposite ends of a magnet

prediction: what you think will happen in the future

repel: to push away

Index

Log on to www.av2books.com

AV² by Weigl brings you media enhanced books that support active learning. Go to www.av2books.com, and enter the special code found on page 2 of this book. You will gain access to enriched and enhanced content that supplements and complements this book. Content includes video, audio, weblinks, quizzes, a slide show, and activities.

AV² Online Navigation

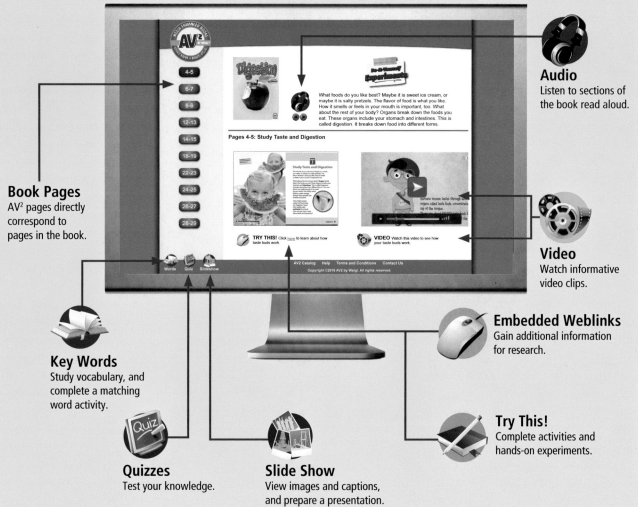

Book Pages
AV² pages directly correspond to pages in the book.

Audio
Listen to sections of the book read aloud.

Video
Watch informative video clips.

Embedded Weblinks
Gain additional information for research.

Key Words
Study vocabulary, and complete a matching word activity.

Try This!
Complete activities and hands-on experiments.

Quizzes
Test your knowledge.

Slide Show
View images and captions, and prepare a presentation.

AV² was built to bridge the gap between print and digital. We encourage you to tell us what you like and what you want to see in the future.

Sign up to be an AV² Ambassador at www.av2books.com/ambassador.